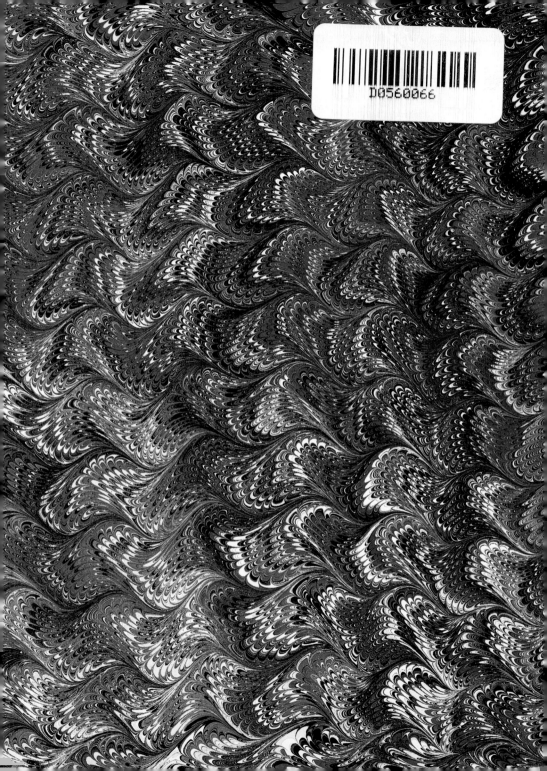

D0560066

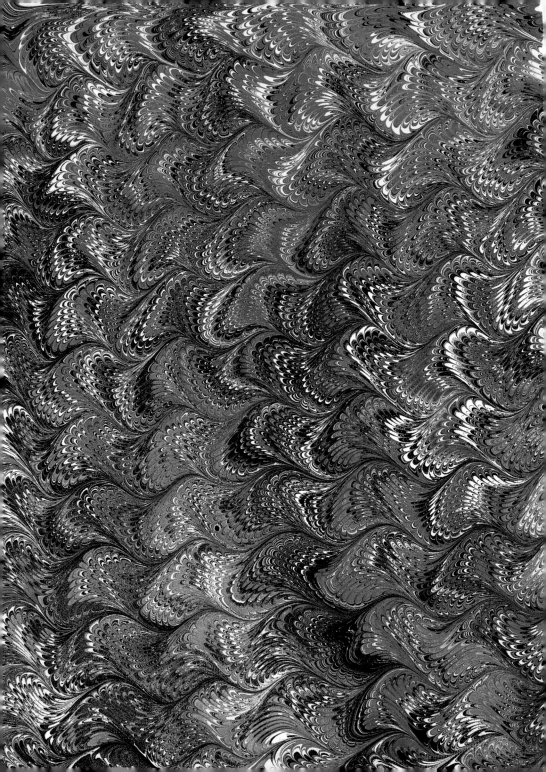

THE TRAVELS OF
LADY "BULLDOG" BURTON

THE TRAVELS OF
LADY "BULLDOG" BURTON

SANDI TOKSVIG

AND

SANDY NIGHTINGALE

LITTLE, BROWN

A Little, Brown Book

First published in Great Britain in 2002 by Little, Brown

Text copyright © Sandi Toksvig 2002
Illustrations copyright © Sandy Nightingale 2002

Map: James Stanford
Courtesy of the London Library

The moral right of the authors has been asserted.

All rights reserved. No part of this publication may be reproduced, stored in a retrieval system, or transmitted, in any form or by any means, without the prior permission in writing of the publisher, nor be otherwise circulated in any form of binding or cover other than that in which it is published and without a similar condition including this condition being imposed on the subsequent purchaser.

A CIP catalogue record for this book is available from the British Library.

ISBN 0 316 86007 7

Design and art direction by Gary Day-Ellison
(www.Day-Ellison.com)

Printed and bound in Great Britain by Butler & Tanner

Little, Brown
An imprint of
Time Warner Books UK
Brettenham House
Lancaster Place
London WC2E 7EN

www.TimeWarnerBooks.co.uk

CONTENTS

August, 2002
The British Library
London

Gentle Reader,

The challenge of bringing Lady "Bulldog" Burton's writing to a new and wider audience has been a formidable one. Who among us can say that their modern lives have not been touched by this redoubtable Victorian lady? I would like to claim that her papers fell into my hands through diligence and intense academic study. However, I feel the truth must out or, in the words of Lady B herself, "I am bound to be tripped out of the hot-air balloon of a lie into the earthly chasm of truth whilst indulging in a glass of claret."

I came across her neglected journals among the hallowed shelves of the British Library during research into another matter. I had thought to pen a post-colonial novel set in Gabarone, the capital of Botswana. The book was to be centred around a convent and was temporarily titled *The Nuns of Gabarone*. As I searched for *The Big Book of Botswana* on the lower shelves of the King's Library, I came across a small bundle wrapped in a silk garter and a chamois leather from a garage in East Horsley. It had lain undiscovered for some years between a first edition of *Essential Commands to Servants in Swahili* and a rather inferior copy of Agatha Philbeam's *Guide to Devotional Kneelers 1678–1679 (not November)*.

The papers were in a poor state but I was instantly gripped by the unique story of an inveterate traveller who did so much to spread the influence of British civilisation throughout the empire towards the end of the nineteeth century. How blessed we have been also to secure the original paintings and sketches by Lady Burton's companion Jinks. These have been painstakingly restored by my collaborator Sandy Nightingale, whose hours with a sable-hair brush have frankly taken their toll.

I trust you will find the enterprise worthwhile.

Sandi Toksvig (signature)

Sandi Toksvig

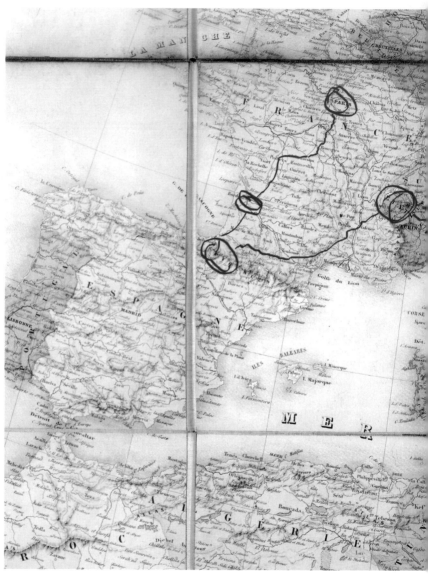

Map used by Lady "Bulldog" Burton to chart her travels. Inexplicably, it appears to have been torn from a book belonging to the London Library.

Paris to Bordeaux, France

June 9, 1880

Heading south from "Gay Paree" and, indeed, to a large extent it was. Jinks, however, not at all well. I was loath to depart our delightful bolthole in Montmartre as my lessons in the art of *le cancan* had, I felt, revealed a hitherto unrealised aptitude. Jinks's chest has been a shocker since that regrettable incident with the young woman from the Folies Bergère, the merkin* and Lord Bartlett (minus his spectacles – a fact which I feel was under-reported in *Le Monde*). I am fairly confident that anyone attacked by a merkin ejected at high speed would have had a similar reaction. The entire affair was not assisted by the woman beside Lord Bartlett who I believe thought it was a cat. The whole matter was a misunderstanding which should never have been put into the hands of the local judiciary.

---

* Ed. Note – It seems a merkin is false hair used to cover the nether regions. A toupee, if you like, for the privates. Despite consultation with the Curator of Underwear at the Victoria and Albert Museum, I regret that I am still somewhat hazy as to its method of attachment.

CARTE POSTALE

ADRESSE

Messrs Fortnum
and Mason,
181 Piccadilly,
London,
Angleterre.

Kindly send 2 partridges
(half a crown each) &
half stuffed pheasant,
whole stuffed Ambassador's
(15/-) care of Ambassador's
residence. DO NOT Label
F & M due temptation
to pilferers.
Lady Bulldog Burton

Mackenzie,
Albion Street,
London,
Angleterre.

Truly

Jinks met an artist called Manet in the F-B bar, and showed him this sketch of me. He seemed impressed.

Jinks has been gulping Ayers Cherry Pectoral *("Cures colds, coughs and all diseases of the throat and lungs")* with the gusto of a rabid horse at water, but, alas, to no avail. She heaved and wheezed until people suspected that I was sharing my rooms with an asthmatic goose. I did attempt a brief stint à la Florence Nightingale. I thought the costume fetching but when I tried to soothe my companion's fevered brow she would keep projecting and spraying. It was with some regret that I realised, with or without the aid of a stout linen handkerchief, I simply cannot "do" moisture. We left the city on a cloud of infection.

Highlight of the trip to Paris

Had tea at Victor Hugo's place on the Avenue d'Eylau. He is lately returned from exile in Brussels (I've never been but I hear the return was wise), where I believe he was given his marching orders for housing socialists. Ever one to put on a broadminded hat, I went anyway. The poor man, however, is not at all what he was and, sadly, is now stricken with cerebral congestion. Priding myself on overlooking such shortcomings, I tried various topics but there was no conversation in him. I even thought to discuss that commune business of a few years ago, but I confess I was a little hazy on detail. As I understand it the people wanted a different calendar, no more church and to stop bankers working at night, which I think tells you everything you need to know about that class of person.

Even Mr. Hugo's excellent companion Juliette says he is most odd now. Apparently he often greets visitors by *singing* excerpts from his novel *Les Misèrables*! Understandably this drives them from the room before so much as a sherry has been poured. His daughter Adele, of course, eloped to America some years ago, only to return certifiably insane. It is, I believe, not an uncommon experience.

In general the food in Paris has improved, considering it is less than ten years since the people of the city were forced to eat the population of the zoo. (I understand eland to be palatable but they say there is almost nothing of edible value on a parakeet.) Always interesting to speculate – if it weren't for the invention of sturdy iron cages things might so easily have been the other way round.

Baron Haussmann has made quite a difference to the cities. Boulevards all over the place and they say the sewers make the rats proud. I was offered a tour but I am of the firm opinion that it is vulgar to venture underground until required to do so in a box.

After our aborted tea with the Hugos, Jinks insisted on visiting the Père-Lachaise Cemetery. Here, in the north-east corner, one can view the Mur des Fédérés, the federalists' wall, where 147 members of the commune were shot and then buried where they fell. The nearby café serves a perfectly respectable scone.

* Ed.Note – Few recipes from the great eating of the zoo have survived. *Nerfs de Daim*, a soup made from the sinews of the Axis deer was said to be high in flavour and gelatinous but "took a monstrous deal of boiling". *Tripang* or Japanese sea-slug strongly divided opinion, with some declaring it unpalatable and others eating it with delight, saying it was the near equal of turtle. Kangeroo ham was terribly salty and not very tender while the *Ris de veau à l'oseille de Dominique* was gone in a moment.

En route to Bordeaux

By great good fortune, as we travelled south, we chanced upon Lady Julia Charles (One of the Chelsea Charleses and the author of *Three Years Spent Wandering in the Northern Provinces of China with but a Single Valet*), and she instantly pronounced the cure.

We alighted at Bordeaux and were advised to prepare ourselves for an evening perambulation. Unsure of our intended destination and mindful of Jinks's health, I wore my warmest cloak while she merely carried my absolute essentials in a small portmanteau.

Holding a dim oil lamp and a large stick, Lady Charles led us with some boldness, and in the dark of night, through the back streets near the Garonne River until we arrived at a low den of her acquaintance.

A small Oriental gentleman gave us admission and I knew in an instant where we had arrived.

"*Une fumerie d'opium Chinoise!*" I gasped. "A Chinese opium den," I whispered to Jinks, whose French, frankly, is no better than one could hope for. Lady Charles nodded. I was in a state of some horror. We had arrived in a lair of iniquity, the haven of the poppy, the haunt of the *fleur de mort.*

A small Chinese woman persuaded us into silk pyjamas of the Orient whilst I continued to make some protestation.

"But my dear Lady Charles, opium smoking cannot be condoned. It is known to throw whole families into ruin, dissipate every kind of property and quite likely ruin man himself."

"True," she replied sagely, "but Jinks's cough is very bad."

It is the burden of the employer that one must occasionally march the road of discomfort for one's charges. Knowing the gift of the poppy as a universal cough suppressant, I felt I had no choice but to soldier on. Seeking only the health of my devoted companion I allowed our descent into the smoking room.

Slavish to a firm belief in the maxim "Anything worth doing is worth doing well", I will pass on to you that opium is most efficiently smoked in the reclining position. We lay on large divans in the silk-lined room whilst a chef prepared "*L'allumage de la pipe*". For reasons I cannot quite fathom, I regret that I have scant detail about the remainder of the evening. I do recall that the pipe has a considerable odour. Not unpleasant but rather creamy.

Lady Charles, normally a woman of some fortitude, seemed quite glass-eyed with the enterprise. Indeed, her familiarity with the entire operation suggested a constitution regularly racked with consumptive coughing.

The effect on Jinks was singular. Her rather poor French improved dramatically. I think she was still under the weather though, for she was eventually carried from the cellar crying, "*L'esprit des Buddhas morts habite dans mon cervau.*" ("The spirit of dead Buddhas live in my brain.")

Lady Charles seemed unperturbed. "Really, my dear?" she said, grasping Jinks by the ankles. "I dreamt I was an odalisque and it was heavenly."

Suffice to say, I cannot help but recommend the enterprise. Jinks's cough is entirely cleared and we depart on the morn for Bayonne.

PAMPLONA, SPAIN

July 7, 1880

If I have learnt a lesson in travelling to Spain, albeit briefly, it is:

1. Not to go again.

2. Never to trust an inferior guidebook.

Unable to locate either a Murray or a Baedeker guide to the region I was reduced to the words of wisdom of one Henry O'Shea. I should have been suspicious that Mr. Baedeker did not even think the area worthy of publication. Although Mr. O'Shea's ruminations are allegedly published in Edinburgh, their superficial and misleading character suggest to me that he is perhaps an Australian.

We arrived by train from Bayonne. Bordeaux to Bayonne (6 hours on the omnibus train). Bayonne to Alsasua – a station on the Madrid and Burgos Railway (5 hours 30 minutes). Then Alsasua to Pamplona (2 hours) on a line

belonging to the Grand Central – owner, M. M. Rothschild. (Why rich men with no knowledge of catering must dabble in railways confounds me. The buffet is hideously inferior.) The *ferro carriles* (railway) passes through no town of importance although it crosses several very picturesque valleys watered by the Borunda and other minor streams. Soon after Zuaste we reached Pamplona (pop. 22,896 – each and every one of them, I feel, not entirely well).

Stayed at a small inn called the Fonda de Europa, which can be found in the Paseo de Valencia. Here they serve endless *carne cocida* (boiled meat) for the *mesa rodonda* (table d'hôte). I realise that I now know the words for boiled meat in six languages – and don't care for it in any of them.

History of the city

Originally called Pompeiopolis or Pompey's City, having been founded by Mr. Pompey himself in 75 BC. This was corrupted by the Moors to Banbalunah, which I think is less of a corruption and more a disgraceful lack of attention to spelling. Before that it was called Iruña, which in the local Basque language simply means "The City". Patently a place of no discernible character, it is the capital of the Navarre district. Not a promising citadel. A sort of 1400-foot-high boil on a fertile plain of the Agra River, squeezed within a tight girdle of walls.

For reasons I can't fathom it has been much fought over. The Arabs went backwards and forwards for years, then the Vascones took charge. Charlemagne popped in for a bit and burnt the walls, which was not popular so he left. Back came the Moors with more matches. All very tense with lots of fighting. It made everyone quite upset. Indeed, one wounded captain (I have no idea on which side) became quite deranged and stayed on to found the Jesuits. I can't believe they are an entirely bright people. Apparently, in 1808, a group of French grenadiers with occupation on their minds started a snowball fight outside the city walls, whereupon the people came to watch and the French grabbed the drawbridges and took the town. An obvious ruse to my thinking.

Pompey the Great

I must confess to having little patience with the details of history but I quite took to what little I read of Pompey the Great. Such a nice title for a start. You know where you are with a name like that. One would feel confident in dispatching a dinner invitation to anyone called Something the Great. His real name was Gnaeus Pompeius Magnus, which I think is less successful and you can see why a change was necessary.

He was born in 106 BC, which is practically before any of my friends. Naturally he came from money, albeit Roman money, which I realise no one would count as much. He joined the army – so useful for a young man wanting to travel – and traipsed all over Europe in his sandals and white sheet of a dress. He was obviously a good sort. They say he cleared the sea of pirates in three months. What splendid fun. It all went wrong in the end and the Egyptians cut off his head. I haven't tried Egypt yet, but Jinks and I shall certainly approach the place with caution and something stout tied around the neck.

The Cathedral is the principal sight of Pamplona. It was built in 1397 by Charles the Noble, although presumably not on his own. He and his wife, Queen Leonora de Trastâmara, are entombed inside. He with a lion at his feet, she with two dogs, and both with the largest noses I have witnessed hewn from marble. I cannot help but feel the sculptor, one Jean de Loome of Tournai, was a confident fellow either not in need of further royal patronage or simply desirous of somewhere to hang his hat.

Ed. Note – Jinks's sketch of the tomb of Charles the Noble differs in many respects from the actual memorial. While not wishing to cast doubt on Jinks's involvement in Lady B's Grand Tour, it is almost as though she never saw the monument.

Souvenirs

Jinks has developed a positive passion for the irritating habit of the souvenir. I find it vulgar to collect the detritus of foreign climes, but she will not be swayed from her purpose. There is a Lord Elgin fever about her desire to return home with half of Europe by her side. Her latest acquisition is a pair of castanets. (From the Spanish *castañuelas*, diminutive of *castaño* or chestnut. My Spanish is proceeding apace although I have yet to find anyone I wish to converse with.) These hollowed-out pieces of wood are designed to sit in the hand and be clapped together as a musical instrument. So far Jinks has not proved adept at this and, indeed, her right-hand index finger has swollen to alarming proportions. They say the Romans played something similar called *crótalo*. I begin to suspect it was the undoing of Pompey in Egypt.

I had come to Spain with the vague notion of furthering my interest in dances of the Continent. I was not sure if this would be possible. The wretched Mr. O'Shea assured me that, "Pamplona is very dull and the only amusement is on the tennis courts."

I must say I consider tennis to be undignified and venture to suggest that it will never be a sport for the English to excel at.

It was with the flamenco in mind that I ventured out just after 7.30 one morning from my inn where meat boiling began at a surprisingly early hour. Dressed in a rather brilliant red cloak (I have often found colour a good calling card with native peoples), I set forth for my *paseitos* (Spanish stroll) with some excitement. I should tell you that pedestrianism is unknown in Spain and scarcely to be thought of. Consequently I was surprised when, wandering along the Cuesta de San Domingo, I noticed quite a gathering of men and young boys catching the morning air.

"*Encierro!*" they called to me. "*Encierro!*"

"And a very good morning to you," I replied, enjoying the local exchange. Spanish is a tricky tongue and I have only a few essential phrases but thought

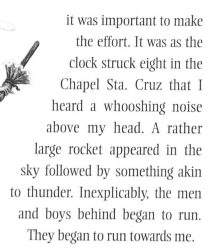

it was important to make the effort. It was as the clock struck eight in the Chapel Sta. Cruz that I heard a whooshing noise above my head. A rather large rocket appeared in the sky followed by something akin to thunder. Inexplicably, the men and boys behind began to run. They began to run towards me.

Brigands! I thought. The entire town is composed of brigands. When confronted by immediate danger an Englishwoman has only one choice – to face the onslaught and recall the many uses of a properly projected parasol. It was as I turned that I noticed the second rocket and, indeed, the bulls.

I have the same fondness for animals that any woman of breeding might adopt. I believe they can be charming, but become less so the nearer they are to you and the further from a plate. Behind the fast-approaching mob of males was an even speedier collection of bovines. Rather cross bovines. At a quick

guess I would have said each thundering bundle of muscle and fury weighed
some 1200 pounds, but it was not a moment to stop and ruminate. The men
ran, the bulls ran, and, indeed, forsaking all propriety, I began to run. Down
the Mercaderes and Estafeta roads and into the bullring.

I suspect my fitness resulting from arduous attention to the can-can may
offer some explanation for my arrival ahead of both mob and mad *biche*. In the
ring of the toreadors, the bulls were swept into an enclosure and I
found myself much cheered by the local populace who had
gathered rather as artisans do
on Derby Day.

The *autoridad* in charge was most gracious. Apparently, this "run with the bulls" has been an annual event since the sixteenth century. Not only was I the first woman to have participated but also the first *inglesa* to have made such a good show of it. Before the bull fighting proper began, he said a few words that sounded lovely but could have meant

anything, so I gave a short reply in Spanish which began rather confidently

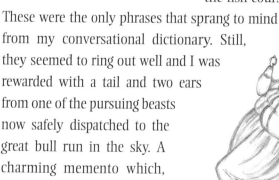

with a ringing *"El pueblo de Pamplona . . . "* and then deteriorated into declarations that I knew where the post office was, that my linen had not been returned from the laundry and that the wine for the fish course was most clearly corked.

These were the only phrases that sprang to mind from my conversational dictionary. Still, they seemed to ring out well and I was rewarded with a tail and two ears from one of the pursuing beasts now safely dispatched to the great bull run in the sky. A charming memento which, sadly, began to smell in our luggage and which Jinks threw from our train compartment as we traversed a viaduct.

We were escorted to the railway station by a mêlée of *picadors*, *banderilleros* and *espadas* who pleaded with us to endure another day of the fiesta. We declined and headed north as fast as possible. A charming peasant people but I venture to suggest that no Englishwoman in her right mind will ever voluntarily spend leisure time south of the Pyrénées.

Ed. Note – Los Sanfermines:
The bull-running fiesta (overlooked by Mr. O'Shea in his preoccupation with tennis courts) celebrates one Saint Fermin. He was, apparently, the son of a Roman senator and the first Bishop of Pamplona. Fermin was consecrated by San Saturnino who was martyred by being dragged about by a bull. Fermin himself travelled to the Gauls as a missionary and was beheaded in Amiens for his trouble. Lady Burton believed that such stories explained why England is so low on producing saints. In a scrap of correspondence I have found to her milliner complaining of the poor quality of ostrich feathers, she also ruminated on Fermin's troubles with the bull and eventual beheading. She wrote, "I cannot imagine such an event occurring anywhere in Britain and certainly not in the Home Counties where people might hear of it."

Critical Spanish phrases

¿Dónde está el correo? – Where is the post office?

¿Qué calor? – Isn't it warm?

Encierro – The running of the bulls.

¡Corvé, tonto! – Run, you fool.

Disculde joven, pensé que usted llevaba una sombrilla –
I am so sorry, young man, I thought you were carrying a parasol.

¿Tiene usted uno con imagen de la Virgen Maria? –
Have you got one with the Virgin Mary on?

No sea absurda, soy Inglés – Don't be absurd, I'm English.

Mosquito – Mosquito.

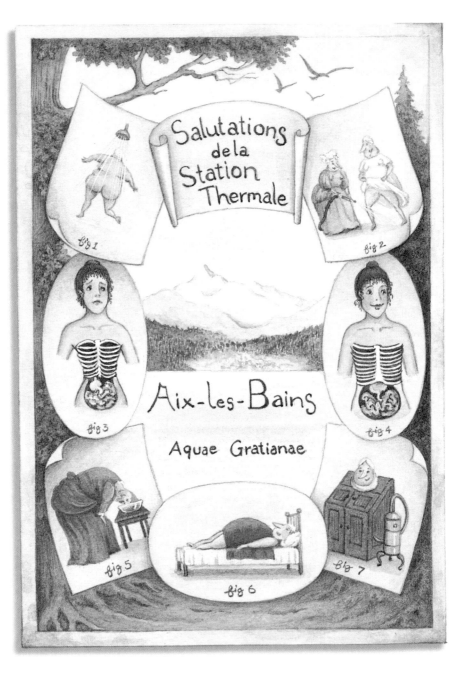

AIX-LES-BAINS, FRANCE

July 31, 1880

I am sometimes given to wonder why I travel with Jinks at all. While it useful to have someone who can sort my collars and cuffs and cord the luggage, I am not at all sure it is always worth the trouble. I have explained to her that were it not for my kindness she might have to suffer the degradation of becoming, heaven forfend, a governess, but the remarks seem to fall on stony ground.

Our trip to Aix-les-Bains has been memorable thanks in large part to the presence of Miss Phillipa Dennell of the United States. It is a sad fact that pretty young women abroad often have to change hotels when young gentlemen tourists become too attentive. Without wishing to be unkind, it gives you some idea of the challenge Miss Dennell presented to the world, that upon our arrival at the Hôtel de France we found she had resided in the same room for some months with no trouble at all. We had arrived at the behest of our dear Lady Charles, who had strongly advised us to take the waters and to avoid Miss Dennell at all costs.

"She is a bluestocking of quite the worst kind. Not only unconventional but untidy. She rides the omnibus any old how and has been known to sit in the lounge talking for hours with her feet on the fender."

The place was awash with the English come to "take the cure". They limped about amusing themselves by referring to the town as *Aches and Pains* and they smelt relentlessly of sulphur. Not an odour which even the most ardent user of imported toilet soap can carry off with aplomb. Jinks did not want any treatments. She said she had grave scruples about all medical interference. I have to say that upon arrival in the town I felt absolutely fine, but after a single consultation began to have some doubts about my health. The bill alone made me feel queasy in the extreme.

Our dinner table was a curious mix. There was "Dr." David Young of Guildford in Surrey. A retired major from the Army, he had been in the area for some time. He spent his days practising doctoring on the local peasants. He was not a real doctor, never having studied medicine, but there was a general consensus that what he lacked in expertise he certainly made up for in kindness. His advanced deafness made him a slightly tiresome dinner companion and did make one fret somewhat for any patient attempting to relate the exact nature of their complaint.

A mother and daughter, Mrs. Archibald Wright and Miss Louise Wright, also joined us at dinner. Mrs. Wright was a woman of immense proportion whom no one wanted

to sit next to as she entirely blocked any hope of a view from the dining-room window.

By simply leaning forward she was perfectly capable of obscuring a complete condiment set for the entire meal.

Her daughter, Miss Wright, was of a nervous disposition, her principal aim in life to retire to a reclining position on a sofa. Her mama declined this solution and had placed her child on a strange course of treatments. In the main, these seemed to involve standing for an hour each day with her head upside down in a bowl of water, followed by a short session attached to the newly arrived Davis and Kidder Patent Electric-Medical machine. This boxed instrument delivers a series of high-voltage electric shocks through the skin and tissue of patients with "nervous" disorders. After six weeks of this, Miss Wright was now a jibbering wreck who shook incessantly and could never seem to do anything with her hair, which made her a sight at the dinner table and extremely noisy with the cutlery. Miss Dennell, Jinks and myself concluded the party.

Each night was a conversational challenge. Mrs. Wright had been advised to eat only raw

vegetables. The noise of her vast molars sinking down on a carrot is one that will live with me for ever. She seemed to time this mastication to coincide with any remark of interest made by a guest at the table, and her booming crunch was inevitably followed by dear Dr. Young bellowing, "Did someone speak?", while the nervous Miss Wright appeared to play the "Moonlight Sonata" with her knife and fork. Dr. Young, having thus gained the floor, would wander off into rather detailed descriptions of a Bell's Palsy he had once seen. The demeanour of the table never recovered. Miss Dennell was most forthright about the entire business.

"Must you eat only vegetables, Mrs. Wright?" she enquired one particularly tiresome evening.

Mrs. Wright managed to nod and spray small pieces of apple at the same time. "It's for the weight, you see. It will make me thinner."

Miss Dennell shook her head. "I doubt it. Look what it's done for elephants."

Jinks giggled. Miss Dennell was, amongst other things, a woman of independent means. It seems that her brother, James Dennell, had a patent for cigarettes made by machine whose popularity was sweeping the colonies. Following her pachyderm remark she then cleared the dining room by lighting up one of her brother's tobacco sticks. Jinks gawped.

I do not wish to impugn Jinks's character but I feel I must state that her infatuation with Miss Dennell was astonishing. Never one to venture into unkindness, I think it would be fair to say that Miss Dennell was not an attractive woman. Indeed she looked like a personable man – steel-rimmed spectacles, sleek centre-parted hair with her large ears fully exposed and a square jaw. There were in effect three sexes staying at the *hôtel* – men, women and Miss Dennell. You will know the sort of woman I mean when I tell you she had arrived alone on one of those new-fangled bicycles with inflated tyres. No doubt she had taken one look at the mountain ahead and decided to build her strength.

For the armchair traveller, I can tell you that Aix-les-Bains is a pretty place on the shores of Le Bourget Lake at the foot of Mont Revard with a rather fine view of Mont Blanc. People have been dipping their ailments in here since Roman times. Indeed patricians from the Roman Gaule Provincia region came to bathe here, when it was known as Aquae Gratianae. Today one can still bathe in waters which emerge from a tunnel dug in the rock aeons ago. Apparently the underground journey from the opposite side of the lake takes more than thirty years, which seems an awfully long time to run a bath. The place was enlarged some twenty years ago and there is much attention focused on the *douche écossaise* (cold showers) and the newly improved *vaporarium* (steam bath)

I spent several days getting too hot in the *caldarium* and too cold in the *frigidarium*. As to what occurred during my Kneipp Short Wrap, I haven't the will to explain. Jinks seemed to spend her days solely with Miss Dennell and, indeed, at one supper they failed to appear at all. I was in the process of shouting to Dr. Young

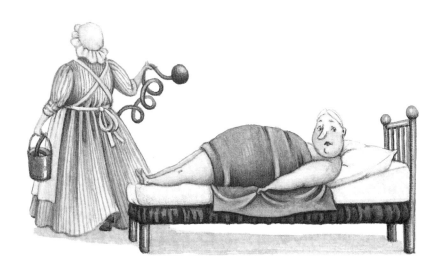

Found scribbled in the margin. Note — to travellers with poor French:
1. Shame on you.
2. Do check which treatments you have actually selected. Some methods of colonic cleansing do not translate well and may surprise.

that I thought perhaps Jinks was unwell when I chanced to see her out of the dining-room window. She was sat astride Miss Dennell's bicycle, who ran alongside, smoking, whilst encircling her arm around my travel companion. I am not a medical expert but both women patently cried out for an immediate *douche écossaise.* Fortunately, Miss Wright chose that moment to have a minor fit, whereupon her mother rose to assist and all views to the mountains were obscured.

I think I would recommend the resort to others. Any aches and pains I had when I arrived were certainly cured, and as for Jinks's scruples, those have entirely disappeared.

CROSSING THE GRAIAN ALPS AT THE LITTLE ST. BERNARD PASS

September 15, 1880

Mrs. Henry Fairfield in her invaluable book *Alpine Byways* says "Without aspiring to exploits which may be deemed unfeminine . . . ladies may now enjoy the wildest scenes of mountain grandeur with comparative ease." I doubt, however, if the literary lady has ever had the pleasure of climbing Mont Cenis. We are in the northern segment of the Western Alps along the French-Italian border, bounded by Mont Cenis and the Cottian Alps (south-west), the Isère and Arc valleys (west), the Little St. Bernard Pass (north) and the Dora Baltea river valley (north-east). Jinks declares that the last name is familiar to her. She is confident that she attended school with a Dora Baltea and cannot think how Dora has come to have a river valley named after her. I used to look at Jinks and marvel at her smooth complexion, but over the years I have come to realise that she has been spared wrinkles by virtue of never having succumbed to heavy thought.

Standing, as it were, with one foot in France and the other in Italy, I cannot decide whether to refer to the mountains as the Alpes Grées or the Alpi Graie and the pass ahead as the Col du Petit-Saint-Bernard or Colle del Piccolo San Bernardo. I think both sound charming and so much nicer than the St. Bernard Pass, which does have a hint of the slavering dog about it.

Many of the white peaks are glacier covered and rise to more than 12,000 feet, each crying out for one to climb higher and higher. We had thought to

climb Mont Cenis before descending to the Piccolo San Bernardo (Italian! I am definitely going with Italian. I feel the language needing to burst forth) and down into the Valle d'Aosta in dear Italy.

We were a curious group. Jinks and myself and, joining us from Aix-les-Bains, Dr. Young and Miss Dennell. In addition, Mrs. Albert Hackett-Fox, the celebrated lepidopterist and botanist, had arrived in a flurry of butterfly nets. She was accompanied by a gentleman whom she claimed as a nephew. He was a simple, smooth-faced boy. It wasn't his age, however, that made the relationship slightly improbable, but the fact that he was, even to my untutored eye, clearly from India. His swarthy looks might have been attributed to the Alpine sun but, even in today's modern times, the wearing of a turban is tricky to dismiss as mere whimsy. Everyone called him Munshi and he spent his time positively staggering under the weight of glass Wardian cases for the transportation of rare species back to England by his "aunt". I cannot quite see the attraction of grubbing about in nature, but I suppose for people who like that sort of thing it is just the sort of thing they like.

Dr. Young also wanted to bring home a souvenir, but being a man he required something large with horns on it. In the pursuit of his mountain chamois he was extremely fussy about his equipment. He hung himself all over with

Mrs Hackett - Fox

cartridges, bags of bullets and powder flasks, tobacco pouches and match boxes, until he resembled a small branch of the John Lewis hunting department. He carried with him a most beautiful rifle.

"Used to belong to the Duke of Devonshire!" he kept repeating, as he polished its gleaming shaft.

I had stripped myself of all adornment for the trip, wearing only a simple Scotch bonnet and a heather mixture tweed jacket which does not show dust and mud stains and yet cannot lose its colour even under a hot sun. Alpenstock in hand, I was prepared. Sadly, Miss Dennell had been seduced by the vulgar vividness of the new chemical dyestuffs. She wore a costume of such brightness that I had no fear for the approach of night on the mountain.

Our guide was an Italian gentleman who had come highly recommended. Signor Liguani was a man of the mountains in whom one could place infinite trust. His neat dark beard covered a smiling face that might have been hewn from the Alpine granite. He wore the traditional garb of the climber but his linen was clean and pressed, which speaks volumes about a person's decency. Even through his fustian jacket one could see the outline of arms formed for physical purpose and with legs which . . .

Whatever his appearance, the charge he suggested for guiding us was most agreeable.

Miss Dennell and Mrs. Hackett-Fox got along supremely. Both women were well travelled and it seems Miss Bonsack had had considerable climbing experience in Thibet. She was pleased to share her mountaineering tips with us which could be mainly

munshi

Dr. Young

summarised thus: "Climbing up beyond the ability to climb down is dangerous," and "Sucking ice and snow merely increases thirst."

Meanwhile, Mrs. Hackett-Fox expounded on the treachery of wild aborigines in the southern hemisphere.

It was a considerable climb. I suppose the Alps cannot help being a big place but there was more to it than I imagined. I had always thought that traversing the Alps meant going up one mountain and coming down the other side. Not so. Signor Liguani contrived to find a whole series of the wretched things, thinking, perhaps, that we couldn't get enough of them. Every time we reached a summit there was another, even higher incline ahead awaiting our attention. I must confess I found it a tiresome business at first.

As we headed for the clouds we passed people living on terms of primeval intimacy with their cows. Miss D and Mrs. H-F examined each native minutely. Mrs. H-F had received a colour chart from the British Association for the Advancement of Science and was most assiduous in holding it against bewildered mountain people so that she might note their skin and eye tone.

"You must be *inglese*," they called as we departed.

It is said that Hannibal led the Carthaginian Army over the St. Bernard pass on his way to Rome in 218 BC. He did so with his legendary elephants, which must have played havoc with the catering. I merely settled for my

S. liguani

invaluable trunk purchased from Edward Cave in Wigmore Street. It is a basket covered with strong tarpaulin which needs no extra cover. It is at once light and impervious to rain and caused Jinks no trouble at all.

We headed higher, dragging up slopes so steep that we sometimes fancied we could rest ourselves against the ground by leaning forward a little. There was much undignified panting and groaning and the occasional tinkle of glass as Munshi dropped another specimen case.

En route, Dr. Young regaled us with the history of the area. It seems that since antiquity the pass has been the principal way over the Alps into Gallia Comata, a province of Gaul. The ancient name is Alpis Graia or "Greek" pass.

"According to legend," said the good doctor, "the Greek hero Hercules, returning from Spain with the oxen of the three-bodied giant Geryon, crossed the Alps by this route."

"Oh, I don't think so," declared Miss Dennell, who has an opinion on everything. "I think that must have occurred in the Maritime Alps."

I suspect, being legend, it didn't occur at all, but failed to interject as Dr. Young had spotted a deer. He raised his precious rifle and fired. Everyone stood waiting for the bang but nothing happened. The rifle was entirely silent. At once we could see why the Duke of Devonshire had so happily parted with his weapon. Dr. Young, being almost completely deaf, seemed not to notice and merely muttered, "Missed. Damn."

We climbed on, thinking no more about it. When we reached a considerable height, the path became too narrow for anything other than single-file passage.

EYE COLOUR AND SKIN TONE
Native peoples of the Italian Alps

fig 1. Makuna thin tri

fig 2. Duithin to tara

fig 3. Apini thescoi

fig 4. Swratn talon

fig 5. Mountain plain

fig 6. Climate to mine

THE BRITISH ASSOCIATION for the ADVANCEMENT of SCIENCE

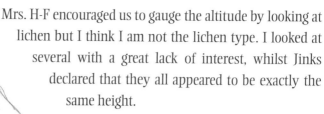
chamois

Mrs. H-F encouraged us to gauge the altitude by looking at lichen but I think I am not the lichen type. I looked at several with a great lack of interest, whilst Jinks declared that they all appeared to be exactly the same height.

Signor Liguani took the lead, followed by myself, Mrs. Hackett-Fox, Munshi, Jinks, the indefatigable Miss Dennell carrying my trunk, and Dr. Young bringing up the rear. It was as we reached a rather glacial ledge that the Duke of Devonshire's rifle finally decided to go off. Signor Liguani had just turned to take my hand when there was a considerable bang. It threw Dr. Young forward into our marching line and produced something of a domino effect.

The ground gave way beneath my feet and the dependable Signor Liguani disappeared entirely from view. Snow and ice cascaded about me and I tumbled for some seconds until I was jerked to a stop. My excellent tweed jacket had caught on the root of a tree and I hung suspended above a narrow ledge. Below me stood Signor Liguani. His firm legs had gripped into a place where no mountain goat could have found a footing. Unfortunately, and this is awkward to relate, the narrowness of the ledge afforded him no movement at all and I, suspended above him, was equally restricted. In the confines of our predicament, my skirts had descended over his head and I could quite feel his breath on the inner part of my knees. Clearly a halt needed to be called and a pause allowed for in which to release tension and recover poise.

(Lillian Campbell Davidson in her excellent tome *Hints to Lady Travellers*, states that a short skirt that clears the ankles is perfectly permissible for mountain work, but the modern costume in which the skirt is merely an inch or two below the knee is hardly consistent with the high ideals of womanhood. From my predicament I think one can see the wisdom of her words.)

Munshi, clinging to an adjacent precipice, was clearly perturbed. He began to chant some of the most striking blasphemy I have ever heard. I don't normally find it appealing but I will say his selection was impressively colourful, original and delivered with finesse. Mrs. H-F, Miss Dennell, Jinks and Dr. Young were still safely on the path, where the doctor was heard to say, "I suspect this rifle wants a service."

It was an understatement of classic magnificence and led me to demand a drink. Mrs. Hackett-Fox passed me a cup from her bag, inscribed with the words *"Temperance is the Parent of Contentment"*, which quite satisfactorily took the entire contents of my brandy flask.

Suffice to say, we stayed in our predicament for some time. Mrs. H-F had with her a copy of Queen Victoria's *Travels in Scotland and Ireland* that she attempted to read from. It might have passed the time had it not been printed in Hindi. Miss Dennell was keen to instruct everyone in the ancient practice of Thumo Reskiang – the ability to raise body temperature through meditation – which she had undertaken as a course in Thibet.

I think I shall never forget the splendid peaks of the snowy range breaking the deep blue sky with their grand outlines as I swung there. Signor Liguani spoke soft Italian words into my calf and it was almost with regret that I spied the rescue party. They had no trouble discovering us for Miss Dennell's vivid clothes stood out sharply against the snow.

They say Leonardo da Vinci tried to climb Mount Rosa on the Italian-Swiss border but stopped his ascent halfway up. He did not know what he missed.

"Clearly, a man of fresco and not al fresco," Miss Dennell remarked. I have to confess I thought it clever.

The poet Petrarch loved climbing. It seems he felt so disgraced by the pleasure it gave him that when he got to the summit he read the confessions of St. Augustine. I thought of this as I hung suspended from my Alp with hot Italian breath beneath and could only recall one phrase from the Saint.

"Da mihi castitatem et continentiam, sed noli modo."
"Give me chastity and continency – but not yet."

At any rate we got home alive, which agreeably surprised everyone.

LAKE MAGGIORE, ITALY

October 11, 1880

There is a general notion that a woman who has over-walked herself is doomed to the day-bed for life. Jinks and I, however, descended from our sojourn in the Alps feeling more refreshed than ever. Indeed, so refreshed did I feel that on our return I gaily dipped my cup in glacier water from the stream, quite ignoring the notion that it is supposed to give you goitre. I am now of the firm opinion that pure, invigorating mountain air is rather less fatiguing than several hours in a stuffy church trying to recall which flying buttress is to be particularly admired. My only advice to the would-be traveller is to avoid descending a slippery glacier. They are irritating beyond all measure to walk down.

Our Alpine adventure concluded with a charming visit to a touring exhibition of lesser-known Italian art masterpieces. Some I thought delightful, while others were clearly lesser known for good reason. Certainly Piero della Francesca's portrait of Eve and her just deserts was poorly executed and I rather preferred the version Jinks sketched for my amusement. Interestingly, both the Italian master and my English servant envisaged the poor wretch in the nude which was a pity.* No wonder she ran away from the garden. In the absence of a good milliner no woman would have stayed.

---

*Ed Note – It is possible that Lady B was making a slight joke here. A "pity" in art is the technical term for a nude. I suspect, however, that she simply thought that a lack of clothing was a shame for anyone.

We have continued on to the Italian Lakes amidst mounting despair over Jinks's ability to read train timetables. She managed to contrive for us to arrive in Turin at a time when even the lowliest *pensione* could not anticipate guests. Consequently, we suffered an unhappy time on a station platform where the only thing one could hope to catch was the influenza. We were not helped by a rather pompous official of the Italian railway. When I pronounced that the departure of the conveyance to the lakes was unsuitable, he responded, "*Si prende si lascia*". My instant ability to translate this into "Take it or leave it" provided scant comfort, so take the train we did.

Thus we set off at the wrong time and in the wrong frame of mind. Despite the fact that I was looking rather fine in my black tailored jacket and jabot in puffed taffeta with draping over the skirt (as well as an excellent pair of Blenheim leather gloves from New Bond Street. My dear friend Lady Joanna assures me that they are quite *de rigeur*), my demeanour, I confess, was less than sunny. Jinks had made no arrangements for our arrival and I fully anticipated greater disaster ahead. It was, therefore, with some surprise that on arrival at Stresa on the shores of Lake Maggiore, we were greeted with rather an astonishing display.

I had been drawn to Maggiore and its Borromean Islands by reading Edward Gibbon – "The fancy is amused by a visit to the Borromean Islands, an enchanted palace, a work of the fairies in the midst of a lake encompassed with mountains, and far removed from the haunts of men."

Ed. Note — Sadly, this picture was damaged during Jinks's conflagration in the *soukh* (see Vol. II. Casablanca).

For reasons that can only be explained by application to a higher Italian authority, the train was delayed. We arrived several hours past schedule which did nothing to improve my mood. Still frowning, I stepped on to the platform to find that the men of the area had not removed themselves at all. If anything they had gathered en masse. I heard a lone cry of, "It is her. You can tell. She is not amused."

Then a thunderous roar of cannon erupted to my left, a volley of trumpets sounded on the right and all around a vast crowd began to shout, while a quite substantial band struck up "God Save the Queen".

Charmed by the local people's attitude to the English, I composed myself and waved to the ensemble. Meanwhile, a young grenadier very kindly picked Jinks up from the track where she had fallen during the first fire of cannon. (She has been reading *The Charge of the Light Brigade* and was, I think, most susceptible to gunfire.)

A military man in a neat moustache presented himself and spoke at length in rather fine Italian. Somewhat deafened by the welcome we had received, I confess I did not entirely hear what he had to say. A dedicated student of Mrs. Humphrey's *Book of Manners*, I resorted to nodding in an agreeable manner and allowing myself to be led along the platform to a carriage. Crowds of charming flag-waving natives lined the streets as we progressed along the shore where a small ferry awaited us. Aware of my responsibility to represent the Empire in as suitable a manner as possible, I acknowledged the greeting with short waves of my hand and the occasional bob of the head.

It was only once we had traversed the waters, arrived at the small island of Isola Bella and entered the Borromean Palace that some idea of the misunderstanding we were under began to surface. Jinks and I were shown to charming quarters; everywhere decorated in the high style with much inlaid

marble, mother-of-pearl, a profusion of carving and a plethora of overstuffed velvet and brocade armchairs and sofas. The military man, one Count Borromeo, bowed low and enquired in thick Italian, "Will it please you if supper is served at eight o'clock, Your Majesty?"

Well, I was ravenous so I said any meal would please me.

"Your Majesty?" repeated Jinks.

The man blushed. "You wish to be incognito. I understand." And then, to our astonishment, he winked broadly and left the room.

To say that Jinks and I were somewhat taken aback would hardly cover the moment.

"He thinks you're the Queen," whispered Jinks.

"Indeed," I said, for there was nothing else to say.

We were presented with a conundrum. To declare our true identity might seem a little remiss at this stage, and yet to continue the charade was . . .

It occurred to me that perhaps Queen Victoria was indeed due in the area. I knew she often travelled quietly abroad as the Countess Balmoral.

"We would be doing her a favour," I said to Jinks. "She can go where she likes now." Thus it was out of duty to my Queen that I decided Jinks and I must suffer the misguided attentions of our genial host. Besides, we were exhausted and had no idea where accommodation might be had at so late an hour.

Dinner was most amusing. The Count had gathered other English people to provide suitable entertainment. These included the Poet Laureate Alfred Tennyson, the zoologist Thomas Huxley and Captain Matthew Webb, the celebrated swimmer of the Channel. Mr. Huxley claimed to be in the throes of studying *medusae* (jellyfish, apparently), but as I believe there are none in the area I suspect he was merely in need of some relaxation. He began to expound

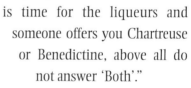

on his published researches about the layer of cells in the root sheath of hair but when I raised my eyebrow at the unsuitable topic he instantly stopped, which was most satisfactory.

Captain Webb then amused us with tales of his swimming. A most determined young man, he had made two attempts at the Channel where anyone else would have failed to consider one. Apparently he was blown off course the first time. The second time he arrived in France after 21 hours and 45 minutes. He had done the whole thing encased in porpoise oil and sipping cod liver oil, beef tea and brandy as he cleaved, breaststroke, through the waves.

I declared it all sounded like too much oil to me and this was deemed to be most amusing. I decided I liked being Queen, as people find your every word the most gripping pronouncement they have ever heard. So engrossed was everyone that I quite forgot some of Mrs. Humphrey's wiser words: "When it is time for the liqueurs and someone offers you Chartreuse or Benedictine, above all do not answer 'Both'."

I confess I did say "Both" – and possibly several times.

Following Captain Webb's tales of covering the channel *au naturel*, a discussion ensued about the recent and absurd suggestion of one day building a tunnel to France under the water. Mr. Huxley quite rightly believed it would be the undoing of Britain, while Mr. Tennyson went quite mad against it. The Count was bemused by this and

it was difficult to tell a foreigner that while people from the Continent are charming in their own way, one does not want them too close.

More wine was poured and, looking back, I suspect the gathering was surprised at how amusing I found the conversation. I think I got away with it, having worked for many hours on my laugh. I would agree that there is nothing more vulgar than the "ha-ha" of the ill-mannered. The proper laugh must be crystal-clear and musical. Once that is accomplished, medical opinion will tell you that laughing is marvellous therapy for the spleen, as well as stimulating the blood and promoting digestion. And why deprive oneself of it, provided that it be truly elegant?

Tennyson and I had a splendid time. He calling me "Queen Rose of the rosebud garden of girls", and I promising to make him a Lord, although I have no idea how this might be achieved.

The remainder of the evening is slightly hazy, although I do recall that

Captain Webb and I swam the distance to Baveno in something of a record time, while the poet and the zoologist shouted encouragement from a small wooden boat. Count Borromeo was aghast at the idea and protested most vehemently. I was, however, Queen, and merely looked him in the eye, declaring, "It is what is happening. *Si prende si lascia*." Splendid.

Lake Maggiore will always have a magic place in my heart. We travel on to Milan with Tennyson's words ringing in my ears.

"So many worlds, so much to do,

So little done, such things to be."

. . . Such things to be. Who would have thought one of them was Queen of England and Empress of India. (We have since had word that Her Majesty's train appeared some ten minutes after our arrival, by which time the town was entirely deserted. I believe she found rooms on the Isola des Pescatori where she learnt more about fishing than could ever have been anticipated.)

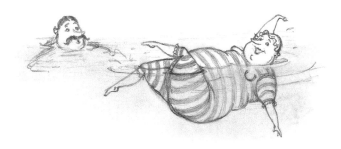

Ed. Note – In March 2000, a statue of Queen Victoria was unveiled outside the Lido Palace Hotel in Baveno, Lake Maggiore. It commemorates Her Majesty's stay in the area. Students of the period will notice a striking resemblance to another traveller of the time.

VENICE, ITALY

December 26, 1880

Wet.

Resting in Venice following our rather exhausting stay in Milan, which I will cover most briefly. I had intended to reside quietly improving my *conversazione* and enjoying *il dolce far niente* ("the sweetness of doing nothing" at which my dear Jinks is an absolute master), when we chanced upon Giuseppe Verdi and his delightful wife, the soprano Giuseppina Strepponi. They were in town for a new production of *La Traviata* where Giuseppina was to give her Violetta. (So curious to find a husband and wife with practically the same first name. I believe it can only confuse the postman.) Giuseppe is working on a new piece based on *Othello* so there was practically no talking to him as he just hums all day. Giuseppina and I had a most interesting time visiting the duomo (founded in 1386 by Gian Galeazzo Visconti who apparently hoped to flatter the Virgin Mary into granting him a male heir. I'm not a scientist but I suspect cold baths and brisk walks would have done more good). The church seats 40,000 and is a barn of a place. It is little wonder that within moments of our visit Giuseppina had taken a chill and quite lost her famous voice.

I shan't go into details, such as the gratifying praise I received, but suffice to say I knew the part of the *Dame aux Camélias* well, Giuseppe had infinite faith in me and I think the people of the Teatro alla Scala (Theatre at the Stairway) gave a pleasing response. I based my consumptive performance on my travels through France with Jinks, and Giuseppe was kind enough to say I achieved something thoroughly tubercular. Everyone sweetly pressed me to stay on, but I felt I had given my all and we departed for Venice on a cloud of flowers, hand-kissing opera lovers and well-wishers. I venture to suggest that the Stazione Centrale will not see the like for years to come.

After such delights Jinks and I have suffered a low moment in our travels. I suppose it cannot all be arias on arrival but the last few weeks have been a trial. I approached Venice quite prepared to be overcome by the beauty of the place and instead have become an ardent admirer of the flea. It is a creature so much cleverer than one might give credit to in the comfort of a Chelsea or Kensington home. I have decided that the skill of fleas lies primarily in the organising of their lives on a military basis. For they work like this:

First an advance party is sent ahead for reconnaissance. This small task-force first establishes one's edibility. Once satisfied that a decent meal is on offer, they send word for the infantry who arrive en masse. These are, of course, merely the forward ranks. Once they have feasted, word then goes out to the camp followers and soon whole flea families descend in an orgy of enjoyment of my all-too-available flesh.

We have now moved *pensione* six times, I have doused the very waters of this damp city with Keating's Insect Powder and yet still the wretched fellows visit me nightly. I believe Baedeker is quite right when he says, "In no country does the treatment which the traveller experiences at hotels vary so much as in Italy and attempts at extortion are probably nowhere as outrageous."

As if the relentless nocturnal munching was not sufficient, I confess that I have also become somewhat irritated with my companion. Since we left the Alps Jinks has barely spoken. When I berated her for her lack of conversation she excused herself by claming she was merely a very "private person". When she found for us yet another hotel where the flea was

fig. 1

52

king, I had to bite my tongue from reminding her that the word "idiot" comes from a Greek root meaning "private person".

I have decided that the idea of cleanliness in Italy is in arrear of the age; the brilliance of the southern climate perhaps, in the opinion of the native, neutralises the dirt. It was whilst dining at a perfectly filthy *trattoria* on the Fondamenta delle Farine that Jinks declared she had solved our lodging difficulties. I was having a ghastly meal, having been given the choice of *testa di vitello* – calf's head – or *costoletta alla minuta* – veal cutlet with calf's ears and truffles – both of which involved pieces of calf that do not belong on the dinner plate. In the end I ordered eggs in the shell, which anyone will tell you is the only truly incorruptible food. Jinks had gone for a walk and returned with the rather bright declaration that our problems were at an end. I was, I confess, ill-tempered through lack of sleep and a profusion of skin irritations, and without thinking I accused her of having taken advice from the *cameriere* (waiter).

I raised my Baedeker and quoted rather forcefully, "'The traveller is regarded by landlords, waiters, drivers, porters and others of the same class as their natural and legitimate prey. If you cannot find the data that you require in this handbook then you can seek further information from fellow travellers, gendarmes, respectably dressed persons present, occasionally from landlords but seldom or never from waiters.' I do not ask the world, my dear Jinks. I simply want an iron bedstead and one night where no other living creature wishes to share my blanket."

Travel can sometimes press the manners of even the most delicate amongst us. I had, I confess, gone too far. My companion sat down and wept. It was an awkward moment. I do not approve of public displays of emotion and yet we had both been strained to the limit. I ordered her a *prosecco* and allowed a pause for reflection. A small street urchin chose this moment to linger near my table. The round face of the child made Jinks smile and she reached into her bag for a coin. Feeling somewhat chastened, I murmured, "My dear Jinks, begging in Italy is rather a trade than a genuine demand for sympathy, and liberality is often a fruitful source of future annoyance and embarrassment." I thought the tears might come again so I gave the child the coin which the waiter had by now failed to secure as his *buona mancia* (tip).

The incident broke the tension and we both smiled.

"It's Miss Dennell," declared Jinks through her subsiding sobs. And indeed

it was Miss Dennell to the rescue. Jinks had stumbled upon her during her perambulations only to find she had secured a most delightful apartment overlooking the Grand Canal. We were swept into her hospitality without discussion. The place is a delight. My iron bedstead is entirely free of inhabitants. Miss Dennell contrived a delightful Christmas for us, complete with the German notion of an indoor tree. Jinks is her old self. I have rarely seen her so gay and contented.

Saluti di Natale
da un Amico

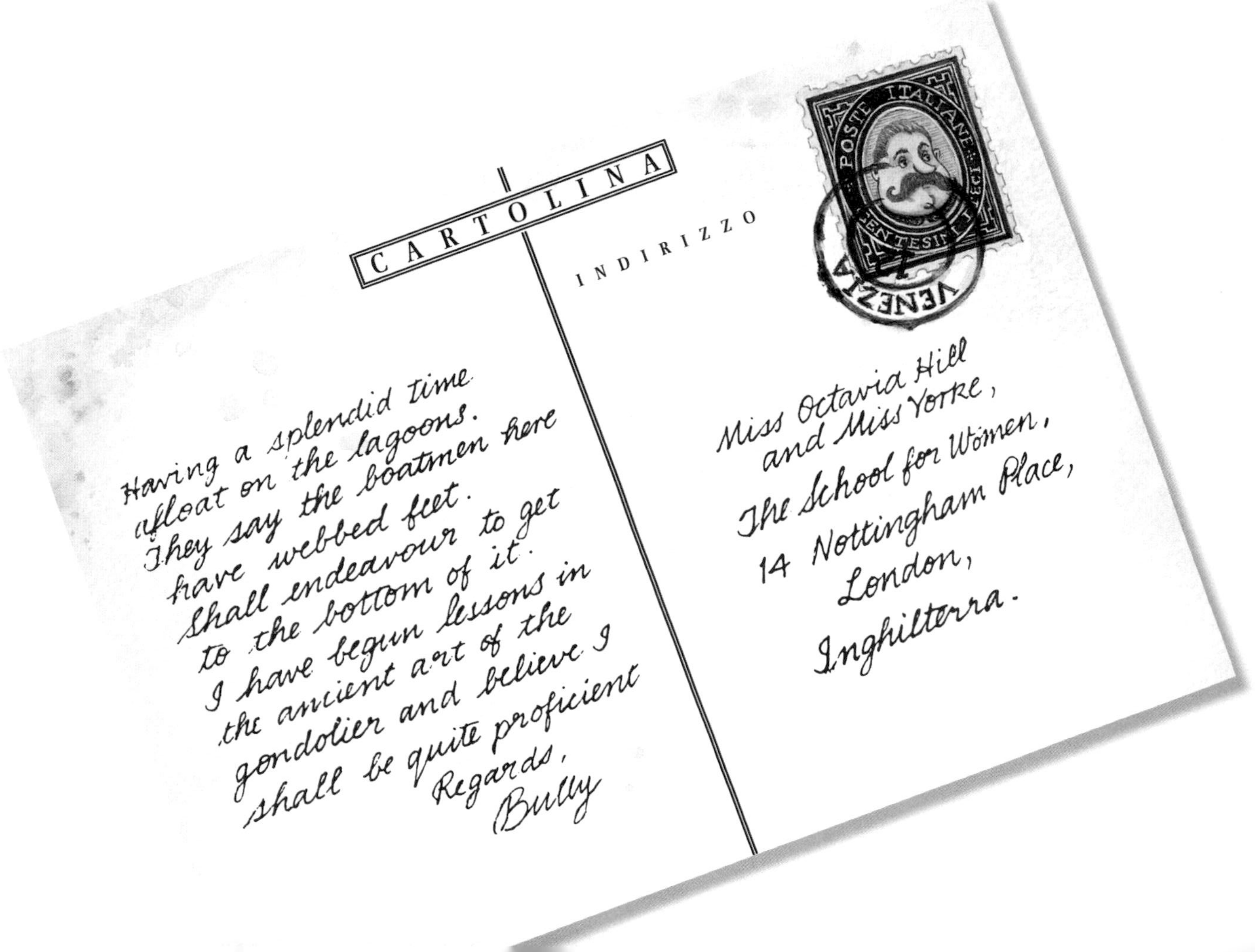

CARTOLINA
INDIRIZZO
POSTE ITALIANE
CENTESIMI
VENEZIA
Having a splendid time
afloat on the lagoons.
They say the boatmen here
have webbed feet.
Shall endeavour to get
to the bottom of it.
I have begun lessons in
the ancient art of the
gondolier and believe I
shall be quite proficient
Regards,
Bully
Miss Octavia Hill
and Miss Yorke,
The School for Women,
14 Nottingham Place,
London,
Inghilterra.

The Carnival

They say Byron threw himself with vigour into the Carnival in Venice but I fear he would have been eclipsed by Jinks and Miss Dennell. The pair appear to have reinvented this pre-Lent extravaganza anew. They go about in masks and gowns, giggling and carrying on as if the very victory against Ulrico, Patriach of Aquileia, was theirs. When costumes were first mooted, I suggested Colombina for Jinks, the malicious yet charming servant girl (Colombina not Jinks). She, however, has plumped for *il medico della peste* (the plague doctor) and runs about town dressed like a demented penguin, poking her beak in everyone's business. Miss Dennell, if anything, is worse. She has selected the costume of *Gnaga* which on the surface looks charming but has a dubious history. It has been described to me as a disguise for young Venetian men in search of rather intense friendships with other young Venetian men. The Turks thought it a disgrace and for once I am with them. Much of the revelry is a mystery to me – men dressed as women, women dressed as men. Apparently in the past men often disguised themselves as women in order to enter convents and commit "*molte disonestá*". I have no idea what that means and no desire to pursue the matter. The Carnival has another ten days to run and I intend to spend them in bed.

ROME, ITALY

Easter 1881

Ed. Note — Sadly, the details of Lady Burton's visit to both Rome and Sicily are scant. The material is badly stained with what was first thought to be blood but may prove to be tomato sauce. Only a fragment of text has so far been restored.

. . . His Holiness said he didn't mind a bit and that at this time of year he had to be at home anyway . . .

. . . The proprietor, Signor Salotto, although an Italian, was most amusing. It was a small establishment where the locals, and indeed many *inglese*, gathered to eat a large disc of flat bread covered with tomato sauce and cheese. This, apparently, is called "*pizza*", which is Italian for pie. There is nothing pie-like about it, but accompanied with a few glasses of Soave it can pass for a meal. Signor Salotto, however, is so enamoured of this dough picnic that he believes it will make his fortune.

"Imagine," he said, "if people didn't even have to come to my restaurant to eat my *pizza*. Imagine if I delivered it straight to their door."

The idea of an Italian turning up at one's door bearing old tomatoes on a piece of bread too depressed even to have risen was too much for my table.

"What a hoot!" declared Miss Dennell. Ever after, Signor Salotto's establishment has become known as the *pizza* hoot and when we are dispirited we hie there immediately.

According to Signor Salotto, the recipe has been in the family for generations. A mural in the establishment showing multitudes of ancient Salottos slaving over flat bread and toppings is said to date from the medieval period. The Signor claims it is by Fra Angelico and was painted many years ago in exchange for dinner for two. Not being an art historian, I cannot vouch for this, although I will say some of the dried tomatoes may have lingered in the place ever since.

SICILY, ITALY

May 3, 1881

Apparently the Greek philosopher Empedocles climbed Mt. Etna and committed suicide by jumping into the volcano. Spent the evening at the delightful English church in Taormina where the rector presented a magic lantern show with spectacular dissolving views of the destruction of Pompeii. I cannot decide whether it was the human tragedy of Pompeii or the departure of Miss Dennell that has left Jinks eyeing the wretched Mt. Etna with Empedoclean thoughts. All I can say is if it continues I may take her up there myself. A fine lemonade is to be had in the gardens of the monastery which welcomes women on Thursday afternoons.

ATHENS, GREECE

June 1, 1881

I hold no ill greater than the sea
To crush a man, how brave so'er he be.

Forgive the classical allusion to Homer, but it seems appropriate as we have just arrived in the Kingdom of Hellas, having suffered a tiresome time in our passage across the Grecian waters. A journey to Greece no longer ranks with those exceptional favours of fortune which fall to the lot of but a few individuals. Athens, thanks to modern railways and steamers, has been brought within four days of London. This is all well and good, but it does present one with a town full of all sorts. We arrived via a small Greek coasting-steamer which was very poorly appointed and, indeed, full of Greeks. In spite of the nominal prohibition, the steerage passengers (who are often more picturesque at a distance than agreeable at close quarters) insisted on invading the after-deck, while the notice forbidding smoking in the saloon was more honoured in the breach than in the observance. The vessel was not so full of life that there was not also room for a host of creatures who wished to share my accommodation. Not only the flea, with which the traveller in Italy has become on more or less familiar terms, but also bedbugs, lice and numerous other disgusting insects, both winged and wingless. I have found that a sleeping bag of linen or cotton cloth tied tightly around the neck will add to comfort but can present difficulties with reading one's Baedeker in bed. Jinks has no head for the sea and her only Greek to date is the word *apópatos* (water-closet). She missed nothing. The food on board was that

deplorable combination – bad and dear. I retired to my cabin where the cries of hoi polloi, the sway of the boat and a rather fierce dose of kaolin and morphine led me to believe that Scylla and Charybdis themselves called me to live among the mermaids of the sea. Not a journey to be repeated.

After docking at Piræus we packed into a fly with another none-too-fragrant passenger from the steamer, whilst the luggage occupied the whole of the exterior. We appeared not so much to be travelling with trunks as inside them. Our arrival at the Hôtel de la Grande Bretagne in the Place de la Constitution was an unhappy occasion. In spite of preparatory telegrams, only one room had been made ready for our accommodation and no other was to be had. Indeed, two persons were sleeping on the billiard table, whilst the ladies' saloon had been converted into an extra dining room. It was neither possible to sit apart from the gentlemen nor to pot a ball without injuring one of them. The hotel contained few tourists but many Greeks called to the capital for politics, pleasure or profit and living *en pension*. It may well be that the hotel is also frequented by English embassy staff as Baedeker suggests, but time abroad has clearly weakened their demands for service. I can only suppose that the unsatisfactory condition of the national finances explains the earnest desire on the part of the staff for receiving tips in exchange for no effort whatsoever.

On first view Greece lacks the variegated charm of a northern landscape, but enjoyment can be found provided one approaches the matter with care. Conscious of the strong Mediterranean sun we headed at first light to the Italian optician Labarbera in rue d'Hermès in the heart of dear Athens to

obtain some smoke-coloured spectacles. Sadly, it was the spectacles which were to prove our undoing. Jinks seemed to think them so fetching that once purchased I could not persuade them from her nose.

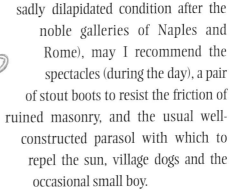

Before setting out to view the antiquities (many in a sadly dilapidated condition after the noble galleries of Naples and Rome), may I recommend the spectacles (during the day), a pair of stout boots to resist the friction of ruined masonry, and the usual well-constructed parasol with which to repel the sun, village dogs and the occasional small boy.

My Greek being classical rather than modern, I hired a local dragoman to be our guide. He was a fine fellow with exceptional English but something of a chip on his shoulder. We headed

out from the hotel and I was immediately struck by the thought that Athens bursts in upon the traveller like a long-forgotten friend. The sense of being at one with ancient times was marred by the guide.

"You know your Lord Elgin?" he enquired.

Jinks, having awoken from her Mt. Etna gloom, was unnecessarily clear in explaining to the young man that despite a passing interlude with Lord Elgin in Bloomsbury (which I felt sure we had

Ed. Note – This piece of cod papyrus was originally thought to have related to Jinks and Lady B's travels in Egypt. (see Vol. II) It was, however, found among the Greek papers and contains an elaborate joke. On closer inspection the left-hand hieroglyphics is a list of Jinks's grievances about her treatment by Lady B at what was a low moment in their relationship in Greece. The right-hand inscription appears to be a note to a kebab shop.

66

agreed never required mentioning again) I do not regard him as "mine". The dragoman, however, was at pains to clarify that he spoke of the political not the personal. It transpires that the Greeks are not thrilled with Lord Elgin and his retention of certain Athenian antiquities behind the columns of the British Museum. I did try to point out that their own treatment of antiquities requires some enlightenment.

"The English government," I explained, "has tried to make amends for its alleged injustice by presenting very handsome casts of all the Elgin marbles to the museum at the Acropolis." The dragoman fell silent and I suspect it is not the way of the natives to acknowledge these little courtesies.

I also suspect that I had made my point, for the dragoman then went to some lengths to make our visit an enjoyable one. He managed to obtain a special *permesso* (5 francs) from M. Kavadias at the Ministry of Religion and Education (88 rue d'Hermès – why not combine the request with a visit to the opticians?) to allow us to visit the Acropolis by moonlight.

That evening, after an unpalatable supper of inedible sheep parts and a rough wine called Kephisia, we passed across the velvety lawn at the centre of the Place de la Constitution as the stars twinkled above the overhanging oranges and oleanders. There were other heady southern trees, all of which

Ed. Note – All road names and prices in the 1880 Baedeker for Athens are quoted in French. This will have aided Lady B whose only real Greek was *mou fénete oloeliniká*.

Jinks either wished to inspect personally or failed to see in her darkened spectacles. The road to the seat of the first Athenian kings wound up between gigantic aloes to the Beulé Gate, which only opened after some prolonged and frankly undignified knocking.

Ah, the Parthenon! That most perfect monument of ancient art. Even in ruins, an imposing and soul-stirring object occupying the culminating point of this plain of Attica. Below us, thin shafts of moonlight shone down upon the Theatre of Dionysus, the very spot that once beheld the birth of ancient drama. I became possessed with the souls of Sophocles, Euripides and Æschylus. Alas, Jinks was I think possessed by the unresined wine from the dinner table.

I began to declaim, I feel quite reasonably, "*Brekekekex koax koax*", the very call of the frogs which Aristophanes understood so well. I could see myself dressed in tunic splendour with a wreath of laurels fresh from some triumph in the Olympic stadia. Jinks, however, did not see at all. In the dim light and behind a darkened lens, she thrust out her arms rather vigorously to join me in the chant and failed to detect a column by her side. The rest, sadly, is now less history than before. It was an impressive crash, with the three full pillars falling in succession to an untidy end – a cannon effect which Jinks has never managed at the billiard table. The dragoman was not as severely injured as he suggested and we managed to depart before the custodian had returned from his supper. Back at the hotel we had time to reflect upon the goodness of Lord Elgin. Just think how much safer everything would have been had he managed to remove the entire Parthenon to London. Despite the obvious rightfulness of our position, we departed Athens at first light.

Essential Greek

Kounoupia – Mosquitoes

Xenodocthi – Inn

Dós mou mía vérga! – Give me a switch!

Lipáme polí aftí i stíli – I'm awfully sorry, but that column is in my way

Ego tha to páro me keftédhes – I'll have mine with meatballs

Qi pósa chrónon aftó? – How old is it?

Proséxete tous Hellenas fernondas dóra – Beware of Greeks bearing gifts

SALZBURG, AUSTRIA

August 23, 1881

Arrived in Salzburg, having suffered an interminable journey from Linz with a gentleman whose conversation indicated that his principal skill in life was that he could cure a smoking chimney using an inflated ox bladder and a stick. It was a small railway compartment made foul by his worship of the goddess nicotine. So smoke-ridden did we become that it occurred to me to beg an ox bladder from the conductor myself. I know the gentleman thought me fastidious but I think he was unaware of the dreadful inflammability of modern female clothing. It is, after all, not that long since Princess Frederick William of Prussia suffered severe burns following the ignition of her dress while she was in the act of sealing a letter, and, indeed, the Countess St. Marsault died when the dress of a companion at a ball in Paris self-combusted. Still, the inflammatory gentleman did consent to share his railway luncheon basket which proved more than adequate.

En route, we passed through the town of Web. Emperor Maximilian the First died here, and looking out I was not the least bit surprised. The Alps of course were very lovely, and few German towns can vie with Salzburg in the beauty of its situation and environs. English and French are spoken at the principal hotels and we found perfectly acceptable rooms at the Goldene Krone in Getreidegasses opposite the house in which Mozart was born. How much more convenient for the tourist when the great of history choose their place of birth near reasonable accommodation. Can I just say, while we are on the subject of Mozart, that although I appreciate his music I do feel sympathy for his parents. How tedious it must have been to have a five-year-old who insisted on endlessly banging away at the pianoforte. Genius is all very well but no one likes a show-off in the family.

All the talk of Salzburg was of the French funambulist or tightrope walker Blondin, who was in Austria for some relaxation. Following his success at both Niagara Falls in the Americas and Crystal Palace in London (where I was privileged almost twenty years ago to see him push a lion in a wheelbarrow across a tightrope whilst fireworks exploded overhead – a curious skill which has not left him in demand for any other kind of employment), every Austrian and English visitor was agog to see if he might cross the Salzach River, here in the heart of town, in a similar manner.

Meanwhile, Jinks has taken to reading the novels of Mary Elizabeth Braddon. She says it makes the trip pass more easily. Miss Braddon (I am confident she must be a 'Miss' for she is certainly "amiss"

in her writing) appears to favour plots which must include bigamy, murder, poisoning, insanity and theft. All matters which I declared we could have found at home and saved ourselves a journey. I dislike the current vogue for the sensational, yet I must confess that I too was not uninterested in meeting the great Blondin. Imagine my delight then when who should we chance upon but the great man himself as we went to dine at the Stiftskeller of St. Peter. (Do try the local beer but on no account attempt the boiled calf's head. It may be that the roof of the mouth is considered a great delicacy but I could not shake the idea that the creature was looking at me whilst I rummaged in its mouth trying to retrieve it. Jinks fared worse, having selected the ribs of the animal for her repast. I believe a lady never looks her best when grappling with a bone and consider that in principle nothing should be sucked or gnawed in public.)

It was not the legendary Blondin who initially caught my eye but his companion, a great bear of a man in a fur coat. Above his lip hung a moustache so large that it appeared not so much to be growing as to have crawled across from one side of his collar to the other. It was a wild animal tamed into place by its owner. It is universally acknowledged that it requires some expertise and practise for a man with a moustache to take soup in a perfectly inoffensive manner. The acquisition of this skill is worth the trouble, for this gentleman ate with an ease which charmed the eye. I do not wish to appear immodest if I venture to suggest that the Honourable Dominick Stimpson was to my

mind a model Englishman. The
consumption of soup was but first
in a catalogue of accomplishments. I
recalled my own dear Lord Burton so
brave in the face of the enemy and so utterly
defeated by a steaming bowl of mulligatawny.

fig 3. Taking soup

The two gentlemen were deep in conversation
about a forthcoming display to be given by the great man of the high wire. It
transpired that the impressive Mr. Stimpson was to present the display but the
pair had arrived at a difficulty. The legendary Blondin wished to carry a
volunteer over the Salzach on his back as he traversed a rope stretched
between the Mönchsberg on the left bank and the Capuzinerberg on the right.
Sadly, it had become apparent to both that Mr. Stimpson, although willing,
was far too substantial a man for the task. I do not recall exactly how it
occurred. Perhaps Jinks, who was reading, gasped when startled by the
moment in *Lady Audley's Secret* where the heroine pushes her husband down
a well to prevent her exposure as a bigamist (I may have glanced at the work),
or perhaps it was my assistance to the landlord in preventing his chimney
from smoking that caused me to draw Mr. Stimpson's cool gaze. Ever
conscious of a lady's ultimate duty to be agreeable I smiled and there it was . . .

Funambulation is a trickier skill to acquire than might be supposed. As it
was generally agreed that the event might attract native admiration, it was
decided that I should perform my part in ethnic dress. The dirndl was fetching
but not very long (the Austrian exhibits little or no fear of the knee). My
principal concern lay with my nether garments. The rope was to be stretched
at some height above the river and my seat upon Mr. Blondin's back might
provide a view of my person that I would not encourage even in the medically
trained. In addition, the valley was not without a prevailing wind and I had no
desire to begin my crossing of the Salzach in triumph and conclude it in the

influenza ward. Jinks and I surveyed the undergarment options in my room. Clearly my cotton pantaloons would be insufficient.

Jinks, who I think was awash with the concept of bigamy and the notion of two being as good as one, declared, "You could wear two pairs of pantaloons," and indeed we tried this. Sadly, the bulk was devastating and quite took away my usually trim figure. It was then, I confess, that I was brilliant. Not two pairs of pantaloons but the parts of two pairs sewn into one. The crossing was triumphant. My modesty was intact, no wind ever whistled in unbidden places and I fell into the beckoning arms of Mr. Stimpson.

Ed. Note — This was the moment of the celebrated double-gusset discovery. There are those who feel that Jinks's part was never fully appreciated.

What is there to say about of the remainder of our sojourn? We strolled along the new ornamental gardens which now embellish the charming riverbank. Below the fortress of Hohensalzburg we stopped at the Ursuline convent and chatted with the nuns. In the land of Mozart, my head became filled with the sound of music. Mr. Stimpson and I climbed the Carolineahöhe, we played amongst the edelweiss and startled a few goats. We . . .

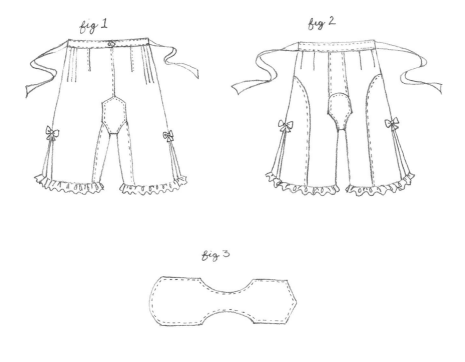

fig 1

fig 2

fig 3

Ed. Note – There are no further entries for Lady Burton's time in Salzburg, although it is known that she and Jinks stayed on till the following Christmas. Certainly it was a happy interlude, but Lady Burton, still nominally married at the time to Lord Burton, may not have felt she could pursue what was obviously the love of her life. Shortly afterwards Dominick Stimpson disappeared. Although he was never seen again, rumours suggest he may have gone to the Americas.

POSTKARTE

ADRESSE

James Smith & Sons,
53 New Oxford Street,
London,
England.

A new parasol
soonest, care of
self, Post Restante.
Silk essential,
parrot head
preferred.
Lady Bulldog Burton

Funambulism

What can I say of tightrope walking that makes the business clearer to the non-participant? The object is to walk on a rope stretched tight between two points. I can't claim to see the point to it and would suggest that the amateur approaches the matter with caution. Many a foolhardy person has attempted to follow in the funambulatory footsteps of Maria Spelterini who crossed the Niagara Gorge just four years ago with baskets tied to her feet. The Great Blondin has, of course, been back and forth across Niagara by rope with the regularity of a number 16 omnibus. I was pleased to discover that his real name is Jean-François Gravelet. I do think Gravelet sounds a rather serious name and I am most surprised his parents ever allowed him to enter into such an absurd profession. Perhaps they failed to occupy the boy, and he was left with nothing but time on his hands and a taut washing-line in the garden.

He is by no means a shy gentleman and he can build a crowd into a positive frenzy. Before the crossing, he and I conjoined on the banks of the river with Blondin shouting to the masses, "Do you believe that I, the Great Blondin, can successfully cross high above this river on a tightrope?"

"We believe, we believe," cried the crowd in a manner I have only previously heard at a rather tawdry religious service outside the Vatican. Blondin kept asking them and they kept yelling. It was really most undignified. At least I was not pushed across in a wheelbarrow or required to eat an omelette halfway. That, I believe, would have been too much.

Useful Remedies for the Traveller

Flatulence

Sulphate of zinc, 10 grams

Rhubarb, powdered, 20 grams

Extract of gentian sufficient to make a mass, which divides into 30 pills, one
to be taken three times a day.

To prevent galling in persons confined to their beds

The white of an egg, beaten to a strong froth, then drop in gradually, whilst
beating, two teaspoonfuls of spirits of wine, put it into a bottle and apply
occasionally with a feather.

Dirty or coarse hands

It is acknowledged by common consent that dirty and coarse hands are
marks of slothfulness and low breeding. No lady should require a remedy.

Consumption

Watercress pounded into a mash and the juice drunk by the patient.

Tender feet

The immediate adoption of worsted stockings.

Electuary for scorbutic eruptions

Peruvian bark powdered, half an ounce

Aromatic confection, half an ounce

Syrup of oranges, a sufficient quantity to mix the bark and confection

Take a piece the size of a nutmeg, three times a day, in a glass of Seidlitz or soda water.

Tooth care

In the summer months tartar may be effectively removed from the teeth by partaking frequently of strawberries.

Colds on the chest

4–6 small onions, boiled and served on buttered toast for supper.

Mosquito bites

Alcohol, either rubbed in or drunk until one no longer notices the itching.

Note from the Editor

The scholar might care to note that there are several volumes of Lady Burton's travel journals, this being merely the first. The rest deal with trips throughout India, Africa, the Americas and points further south. Work is currently underway on the restoration of Volume II which deals principally with the African continent. Miss Nightingale and myself wish to extend our thanks to the British Library and to Viv Redman, a calligraphy expert, who has unravelled some of the more elusive sentences.

Of scientific interest – the stains on much of the paper appear to be a type of gin made only in Venetian bathtubs.

The following short excerpt from the second volume gives some hint of the tales we anticipate in the future.

L'HÔTEL DE FEZ, CASABLANCA

March 21, 1885

Something of a tiresome day although the weather was pleasant. The start was not at all unreasonable – a poached egg and a pot of peppermint tea on the terrace served by a charming man with a monkey. The word for monkey in Moroccan it seems is *bahout,* which I think will prove useful. My perfectly pleasant repast was interrupted by Jinks, who insisted on suffering a conflagration in the *soukh* whilst arranging our luggage for onward transportation. A salutary lesson for her, I think, about just how much paraffin one can safely carry in a small portmanteau.

There was much shouting and carrying on as the local people got quite carried away over a few unexpected flames. I do find the natives engaging but wish they would resist being colourful at an early hour. I, of course, saved the day with a quick dousing of peppermint tea all round. Felt very Joan of Arc amidst the faggots sort of thing. Everyone was very grateful. The little *bahout* clapped around my ankles, whilst the waiter attempted to bring Jinks round. Charming of him, I am sure, but it did mean he quite failed to bring a fresh pot of tea. The end result was much early-morning hysteria (I simply cannot function without my morning cup), my maid's eyebrows flambéed beyond attraction and the loss of a rather fine piece of Louis Vuitton. The singeing of Jinks has blackened her already gloomy countenance into a positive scowl. Indeed, three perfectly acceptable camel drivers have been frightened quite away and I fear we shall be late departing for Marrakech. Ever resourceful, I mixed myself a good stiffener and sent Jinks to the market to buy herself a veil . . .